FAVORITE HORSE BREEDS

AMERICAN QUARTER HORSES

by Cari Meister

AMICUS | AMICUS INK

Amicus High Interest and Amicus Ink are published by Amicus
P.O. Box 227, Mankato, MN 56002
www.amicuspublishing.us

Library of Congress Cataloging-in-Publication Data
Names: Meister, Cari, author.
Title: American Quarter horses / by Cari Meister.
Description: Mankato, Minnesota : Amicus High Interest/Amicus Ink, [2019] | Series: Favorite horse breeds | Includes bibliographical references and index.
Identifiers: CCN 2017019664 (print) | LCCN 2017032229 (ebook) | ISBN 9781681515038 (pdf) | ISBN 9781681514215 (library bound) | ISBN 9781681523415 (pbk.)
Subjects: LCSH: Quarter horse--Juvenile literature. | Horse breeds--Juvenile literature.
Classific tion: LCC SF293.Q3 (ebook) | LCC SF293.Q3 M45 2019 (print) | DDC 636.1/33--dc23
LC record available at https://lccn.loc.gov/2017019664

Photo Credits: Lenkadan/Shutterstock cover, 22; Juniors Bildarchiv GmbH/Alamy Stock Photo 2; Cultura Creative/Alamy Stock Photo 5; Mary Evans Picture Library 6-7; rhyman007/Getty 8-9; Zuzule/iStock 10; mg7/iStock 13; dgphotography/iStock 14; cgbaldauf/iStock 16-17; Rocky Mountain College 18; Carol Walker/Minden 20-21

Editor: Wendy Dieker
Designer: Veronica Scott
Photo Researcher: Holly Young

TABLE OF CONTENTS

A FAMILY HORSE

A horse stands quietly. He loves his family. They brush him. They pick his feet. He is calm. He is gentle. He is an American quarter horse.

A STURDY WORK HORSE

Early Americans used horses for farm work. They needed a sturdy horse. They crossed Spanish and English horses. They got a good work horse.

QUARTER-MILE RACER

Watch out! The quarter horse is fast! It got its name because it ran a quarter mile (402 m) very fast. It was faster than any other breed.

Did You Know?

Quarter horses still win horse races. This horse can run up to 55 miles (88.5 km) per hour!

MANY COLORS

A quarter horse's coat can be many colors. The most common color is **sorrel**. Sorrel horses are a reddish-copper color. Other colors are black, gray, or **bay**.

Did You Know?

Many quarter horses have white star markings on their heads.

A CHANGING COAT

A baby quarter horse is born. She is called a **foal**. Her coat is fuzzy. It will soon shed. Her new coat may be a different color.

RODEO STAR

Quarter horses are strong. They have big muscles. They run fast and turn quickly. They do well in **roping events** at a **rodeo**.

RANCH WORKER

A quarter horse works on a ranch. It helps ranchers move cattle. The horse seems to know where cows will go. It can work hard all day.

Did You Know?

Quarter horses are especially good at cutting cattle. They can learn to get one cow out of a herd.

ROCKY
18 78
BEA

CALM AND FRIENDLY

Quarter horses are friendly. They are calm. They are good for new riders. They sometimes help kids with special needs.

MOST POPULAR

Quarter horses are the most popular **breed** in the United States. These smart and fast horses are good at many things!

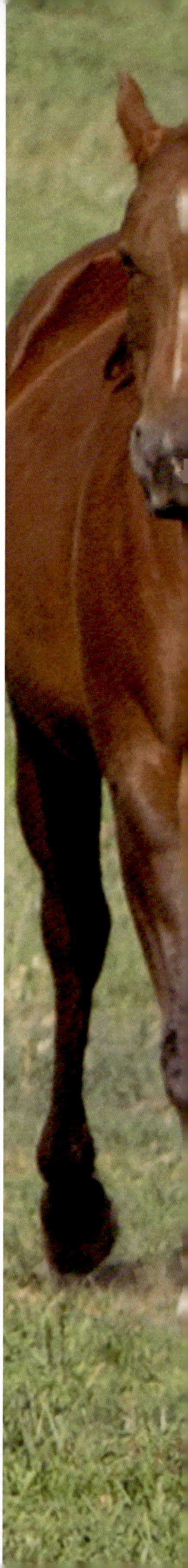

HOW DO YOU KNOW IT'S A QUARTER HORSE?

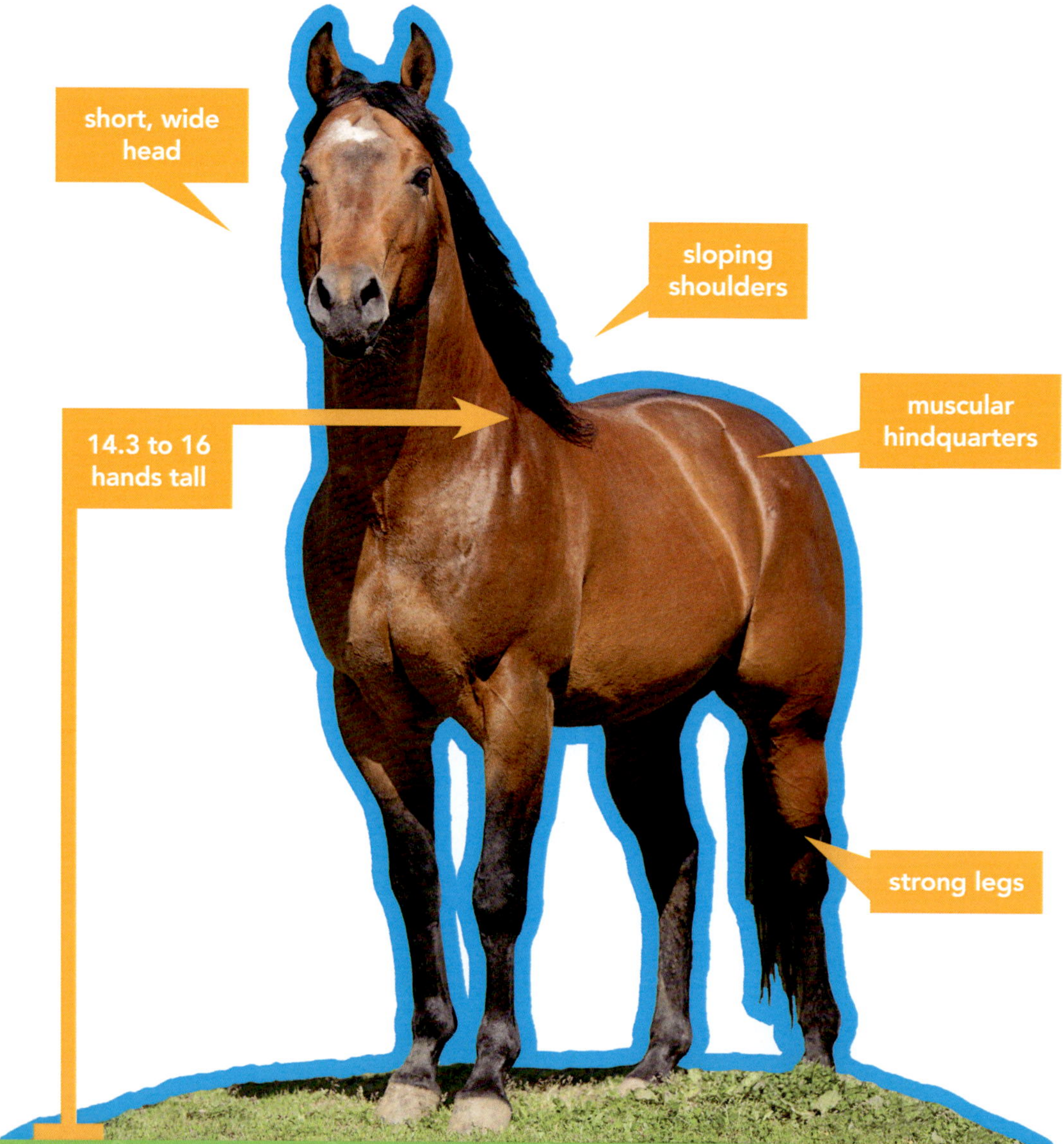

WORDS TO KNOW

bay – a horse color that is brown with a black mane and tail and black ears and legs.

breed – a particular kind of horse that has the same characteristics as the others.

cutting cattle – getting one cow out of a herd and keeping it separate.

foal – a baby horse.

rodeo – a Western horse competition where riders and horses show skills related to handling cattle.

roping event – a competition where people try to catch animals with a rope while riding a horse.

sorrel – a reddish horse color with the same color or lighter tail and mane.

LEARN MORE

Books

Noll, Elizabeth. *Quarter Horses.* Mankato, Minn.: Black Rabbit Books, 2019.

Parise-Peterson, Amanda. *American Quarter Horses.* North Mankato, Minn: Capstone Press, 2018.

Websites

American Quarter Horse | Take Me Riding
http://takemeriding.com/about-horses/breeds/american-quarter-horse

Horse Facts & Worksheets for Kids | Kids Konnect
https://kidskonnect.com/animals/horse/

INDEX